Date Due

MAR 1 7 1989		

💿	PRINTED	IN U. S. A.

Green
Mountain Boy
at Monticello

Green Mountain Boy
at Monticello

A TALK WITH JEFFERSON
IN 1822

by

DANIEL PIERCE THOMPSON

Introduction by HOWARD C. RICE, JR.

Drawings by GILLETT G. GRIFFIN

BRATTLEBORO, VERMONT

THE BOOK CELLAR

1962

✿ Contents ✿

Introduction

Jefferson's Monticello, more than any of the other historic homes of America, still conveys a feeling of the personal presence of its former owner. Caught for a moment by the magnificent setting of the place itself and charmed by the soft speech and proprietorial manner of the amiable hostesses and guides, the visitor feels that "Mr. Jefferson" belongs to Virginia in a very special and almost exclusive way. That is, until the twangs and drawls and polyglot accents of the other visitors remind one that Jefferson, even in his own lifetime, belonged not to Virginia alone, but to the rest of his country and the world at large. This was not only because he had occupied the highest offices that his countrymen could bestow, but because he represented a man of multiple achievements, a "philosopher," in the older sense of the term, whose mind encompassed all phases of human activity.

Speaking of the many visitors to Monticello during the years of Jefferson's retirement, one of his granddaughters recalled: "We had persons from abroad, from all the States of the Union, from every part of the State, men, women, and children. In short, almost every day for at least eight months of the year, brought its contingent of guests. People of wealth, fashion, men in office, professional men military and civil, lawyers, doctors, Protestant clergymen, Catholic priests, members of Congress, foreign ministers, missionaries, Indian agents, tourists, travellers, artists, strangers, friends. Some came from affection or respect, some from curiosity, some to give or receive advice or instruction, some from idleness, some because others set the example, and very varied, amusing and agreeable was the society afforded by this influx of guests. I have listened to very remarkable conversations carried on round the table, the fireside, or in the summer drawing-room. . . ." The same granddaughter—Ellen Randolph Coolidge, whose marriage to a Bostonian forged an enduring family link between Virginia and New England—also remarked that although Jefferson found pleasure in these visits, he was glad to seek from time to time the comparative seclusion of "Poplar Forest," his other house near Lynchburg, for: "The crowd at Monticello of friends and strangers, of stationary and ever-varying guests, the coming and going, the incessant calls upon his own time and attention, the want of leisure that such a state of things entailed as a necessary consequence, the bustle and hurry of an almost perpetual round of company, wearied and harassed him in the end, whatever pleasure he may have taken, and it was sometimes great, in the society and conversation of his guests."

It was not, however, the weariness and harassment that the visitors remembered—if indeed they were aware of it—but Jefferson's pleasure in their society and conversation. They were in fact so impressed by it that not

3

a few of them recalled and recorded what they had seen and heard at Monticello. Many such "talks with Mr. Jefferson" have survived and have been published from time to time. Taken together, and complementing each other, they form an intimate chronicle which breathes continuing life into what might otherwise remain the empty shell of Jefferson's hilltop home.

Thus it was that a young Vermonter named Daniel Pierce Thompson wound his way up the spiral road to Monticello in the summer of 1822; he was then twenty-six, Jefferson was approaching eighty. Thompson, too, recorded *his* visit, in a notebook or diary which appears now to be lost. His early notes were, however, still in his possession forty years later, when he was an elderly man living in Montpelier, Vermont. From these notes he extracted certain passages which were published in *Harper's New Monthly Magazine* for May, 1863. The selection was evidently made with an eye to current applicability and it is possible that Thompson slightly edited his text for publication. But even when such allowances are made, the conversation has the

4

unmistakable ring of authenticity, with details
that could hardly have been invented, and so
must follow closely the notes taken in 1822.
This "Talk with Mr. Jefferson" was reprinted
in part in John E. Flitcroft's book on Thompson (1929), but since it has remained less well
known than the comparable reminiscences by
other New Englanders—those of George Tick-
nor, Francis Calley Gray, and Daniel Web-
ster, for example—it has seemed worth salvag-
ing in its entirety, as a small addition to the
Jeffersonian garland.

Who was Daniel Pierce Thompson? The
question is a natural and not unexpected one
from Virginians and other non-Vermonters.
Vermonters are supposed to know that he
wrote *The Green Mountain Boys* (1839), an
historical novel often referred to in their
schoolbooks and promotional literature as a
Vermont classic. The chances are, however,
that few present-day Vermonters have actually read it. As with many other so-called
classics, the title is more familiar than the
contents. Thompson's grandson, Charles Miner
Thompson (who will be remembered by some
as the editor of *The Youth's Companion*),

maintained that "at least a part of the reason why every Vermonter is proud of his state is to be found in D. P. Thompson's colorful tales of its early history." The claim takes on added authority when it is recalled that Charles Miner Thompson himself published a rather sober history of Vermont's early years (*Independent Vermont*, 1942), in which he presented a decidedly anti-romantic view of the same period of the state's history which his grandfather had done so much to render glamorous. More recently, Dorothy Canfield Fisher (*Vermont Tradition*, 1953) recalled that all Vermonters of her generation (she was born in 1879) read *The Green Mountain Boys* in their childhood, "greatly enjoying the naïve exaggerated glorification of our ancestors—the marvelous literary digestion of youth untroubled by its extraordinarily turgid, inept style." But, she added, "I am told that now even quite young Vermonters can no longer read it. Certainly any literary-minded American non-Vermont adult would find it an impossible assignment."

To bring the record of changing tastes down a generation further, I may add that although *The Green Mountain Boys, The Rangers* and other D. P. Thompson novels were presented to me at an early age by my grandmother, who presumably thought that they constituted part of what every young Vermonter should know, I cannot recall that I ever actually read them through. They remained (these dreary-looking late reprints) among those books that one rather carelessly assumes one has read because one is expected to have done so. Having now attained years of discretion and detachment, I have explored them afresh and am inclined to be a bit less harsh than Mrs. Fisher. They have local color, some authentic historical atmosphere, and stand up at least as well as some of the lesser novels of J. Fenimore Cooper, with which they are occasionally compared. The female characters are only slightly more incredible than Cooper's heroines; something happens on every page; the "good guys," i.e., the Green Mountain Boys, always win and the dastardly Yorkers get their comeuppance—which is merely the reverse of what happens in Cooper.

When Daniel Pierce Thompson visited Jefferson in 1822 he was of course not yet

Vermont's classic novelist, but an unknown young man, even in his own state. Thompson was not in fact a Vermonter by birth, although he came of a long line of New England forebears. Born in Charlestown, Massachusetts, in 1795, in the shadow of Bunker Hill (one of his grandfathers was killed at Lexington), he migrated with his parents in 1800 to a frontier farm on a branch of the Winooski River in Berlin, a "town" adjacent to Montpelier, the capital of Vermont. "Montpelier," incidentally, was a fashionable eighteenth-century name frequently given to airy country estates (to Madison's home in Virginia, for example); it derived ultimately from the southern French city of Montpellier, which was renowned for its salubrious climate and pure air and as a recuperative resort for weak-lunged Englishmen. Thompson found his way out of the woods to Middlebury College, where he was graduated in 1820 at the age of twenty-four. It was through another Middlebury graduate, a minister and professor at the Virginia Theological Seminary, that young Thompson, like so many other New Englanders of his day, obtained employment as a tutor in a well-to-do Virginia family. Unfortunately little information concerning his sojourn in Virginia has survived. The bulk of Thompson's papers—which might have supplied the deficiency—were lost when his Montpelier house burned some years after his death, as related by his grandson in the sprightly memoir which prefaces Flitcroft's dissertation. About all that is known, therefore, is contained in the statement that Thompson himself contributed to Duyckinck's *Cyclopaedia of American Literature* (1856): "Through the friendship of Professor [Reuel] Keith of Alexandria, D.C., he now obtained an eligible private tutorship in a family in Virginia, in the vicinity of the mansions of the old Ex-Presidents, and so far profited by his opportunities as to procure an admission as attorney and counsellor of the inferior and superior courts of the state. After three or four years of this pleasant life he returned home and opened a law-office in Montpelier."

The remainder of Thompson's life (he died in 1868) was spent largely in Montpelier. In addition to his activity as an antiquarian and popular historical novelist, he pursued his career as a lawyer and public servant. He served as clerk of the Vermont legislature, edited a compilation of Vermont laws, and was Secretary of the State of Vermont from 1853 to 1855. "Judge Thompson" was one of the founders of the Vermont Historical Society, wrote a history of Montpelier, was active in the State Education Society, and for a time owned and edited the *Green Mountain Freeman,* in which he waged a vigorous campaign against negro slavery. The masthead of his newspaper carried a variant of Jefferson's words: "We hold this truth to be self-evident that all men are created equal."

With the hindsight that comes from this knowledge of Thompson's later life it is not hard to see why he was attracted by Jefferson's educational innovations at Charlottesville and why he cherished the memory of his visit to Monticello. It was not a political visit, in the narrow sense of the term, for Jefferson by then had left partisan politics behind. It may now, however, help us to trace the ideological thread that led New England "Republicans" of the Jeffersonian variety, like Thompson and many other Vermonters, into the "Republicanism" of Abraham Lincoln's time.

The preserved record of Thompson's conversation with Mr. Jefferson is meager enough, and makes us regret that there is not more. Did the young Vermonter, as he sat there in the shadow of Monticello's eastern portico, manage to steer the talk to his own state? Had Jefferson consulted his far-reaching memory —or those well-classified papers reposing in his library—he might have told Thompson something of Vermont's early history, of those years when the unpredictable Green Mountain Boys, claiming their own variety of independence from New York and New Hampshire, had been a source of no little concern and exasperation to the members of the Continental Congress who were then striving by united action to achieve independence from Great Britain. In another vein Jefferson might have recalled how, a few years later when he was Minister to France, Governor Sullivan of New Hampshire had obtained for him from the Connecticut valley wilderness the skeleton and skin of a seven-foot moose, with which he proposed to refute Monsieur Buffon's statistics on American quadrupeds. He could have reminded Thompson, too, that when he was Secretary of State in 1791, he had transmitted to Governor Chittenden the official notification of Vermont's admission to the Union, and that his own signature was thus to be found, with those of President Washington and Vice-President John Adams, on the State's "birth certificate." Or again, he might have evoked the brief tour of New England that he and James Madison had made in that same year of 1791. After journeying up the Hudson to Lake George and Lake Champlain they had returned southward via Bennington. The stop there at Dewey's was indeed longer than planned, for it fell upon the Sabbath, when travel was prohibited. Thus, instead of crossing eastward over the Green Mountains to the Connecticut valley, as they had intended, they hurried directly south through Williamstown and the Berkshires. But even blue laws could not arrest Jefferson's inquiring mind. "Botanical objects" were of particular interest to him, especially the sugar maples, in which he saw the potentialities of a valuable home industry, worth developing elsewhere in America. He remained in correspondence with Joseph Fay of Bennington, who sent him maple seeds in the fall. Alas, the soil of Virginia did not "prove friendly," as Fay hoped it would, so that Jefferson's attempts to naturalize the sugar maple at Monticello, pursued for several years, remained unavailing. They had been in Vermont in early June and he had seen there in the woods "an azalea with large clusters of flowers and high pink-fragrance," more thickly set on the branches and of a deeper red than the nudiflora variety with which he was familiar. That was when he had amused himself by writing a letter on birch bark to his daughter Martha (Mrs. Randolph, whose children Thompson mentions seeing at the dinner table). . . .

Jeffersonian reminiscences of Vermont, however, were evidently not what Thompson sought when he was at Monticello in 1822. He was not yet the full-fledged antiquarian, and, quite properly, was mainly concerned with eliciting Jefferson's ideas on education and on the "social revolution," as he termed it, then taking place in Virginia. It was to this part of the conversation in particular that Thompson's mind returned forty years later,

at a time when affairs in Virginia had a peculiar poignancy for him, as they did for all
other Vermonters. Sitting in his Barre Street
home, not far from the portico of the state
capitol, he asked himself the question, "Where
would Mr. Jefferson be found today?", just
as he had asked Mr. Jefferson, so long ago,
"Where would Patrick Henry be found to-
day?"

Such attempts to project into present cir-
cumstances the supposed thinking of past
leaders have become the much-abused com-
monplaces of political campaigns and anni-
versary dinners, and should perhaps be dis-
missed as an idle game. Futile or not, they
nevertheless remain an ever-fascinating exer-
cise for the historian, and indeed for all whose
horizons and friendships transcend the narrow
boundaries of the present. This is in fact what
gives to Thompson's brief recollection its continuing interest. In resurrecting his talk with
Jefferson from his old notes, he—and the edi-
tors of *Harper's Magazine* who saw fit to pub-
lish it in 1863—obviously thought of it as a
tract for the times. A century later, when we
are celebrating the Civil War, often in a ro-

mantic manner reminiscent of Thompson's novels, this less-colored fugitive essay of his may still provoke thought as a tract for other times.

HOWARD C. RICE, JR.

A Talk

with Jefferson

by

DANIEL PIERCE THOMPSON

DURING a sojourn in the Old Dominion in the summer of 1822, wishing to visit the buildings of the University of Virginia, then in the process of erection at Charlottesville, and also to visit their illustrious projector, Mr. Jefferson, at his noted residence on the overlooking elevation of Monticello, I procured a letter of introduction to the superintendent of the works, and, repairing to that village, at once delivered my letter to

19

the gentleman to whom it was directed.

"That is Mr. Jefferson," he said, glancing over the letter, and seeing it included the request of an introduction to that personage —"That is Mr. Jefferson whom you see yonder, taking the chisel from the hand of an Italian sculptor and showing him how to turn a volute of the capital on which he is engaged."

"Why, does Mr. Jefferson go into sculpture in so practical a manner as that?" I asked, in some surprise.

"Yes," was the reply; "yes, often, when he detects faulty work. Indeed we consider him the best workman on the ground. But here he comes. I will introduce you; and when he leaves the place, as he probably is about to do, I will go the rounds of the works with you."

Mr. Jefferson—a tall, straight, sandy-complexioned man, wearing a coat of Virginia cloth, surmounting a buff vest and broadcloth pants—advanced with an elastic step and serene countenance, when I was introduced, and greeted with the sweet, winning smile which so peculiarly distinguished him, and which, doubtless, was one of the secrets of his great personal popularity, and magnetic power over all whom he would conciliate.

"You will dine with me at Monticello to-day, I trust," he said. "I must ride down the river a couple of miles, to see to the repairing of the foundation of my mills there, which the rascally workmen slighted when laid in my absence while in office. But I shall return to meet you at the dinner-table."

So saying, he, though then about eighty years of age, mounted the young blooded horse that was now led up for him with the agility of a boy, and galloped away to his destination.

We will pass over our delightful ride along up the spiral road to the top of the broad, dome-shaped Monticello, the unique mansion that surmounted it, the museum, picture-gallery, and library; and lastly, the plain Virginia dinner, presided over by the distinguished head of the household, and graced by the presence of his interesting grand-children, Master and Misses Randolph. We will pass over all these as foreign to the object of this article, which is to report some of the most remarkable utterances with which we were about to be favored.

As we rose from the dinner-table, Mr. Jefferson led me at once to the eastern portico of the house, which was then just beginning to be thrown into the shade, and bade me be seated, with the remark that he had "finished his labors and studies for the day, and had now nothing to do but talk."

"In examining the plan of our University, with its buildings finished and in progress, you noticed, doubtless, that of the different structures designed for professors' houses, no two are of the same order of architecture; and that these houses are to be at least numerous enough to represent the whole of the five orders. The object of this is to furnish correct models for public buildings and private residences, so that students educated here, or their friends visiting here, may carry away with them, and thus be the means of spreading, a true architectural taste among the people of Virginia."

"You contemplate, I am told, Sir, the establishment of some professorships which are rarely, if ever, to be found in our American colleges."

"Yes, especially one of the Saxon language, a knowledge of which, as the foundation of the English, I deem no less indispensable than that of Greek and Latin. I have put myself in correspondence with several gentlemen in England on the subject, and they have recommended two or three different individuals for this professorship. But so difficult is it, even in England, to find any one a proper judge of the competency of another in this language, and so anxious am I that this post should be well filled, that I resolved I would know something of the language myself before finally engaging any one, that, by a personal examination, I may be enabled to form a pretty safe general judgment of the competency of applicants. And for this purpose I, last spring, procured from England a full set of Saxon elementary books, and have ever since devoted two hours each day to the study of the language; and in a few months more I hope to feel myself prepared to meet such applicants in conference. I design, also, that *all* the professorships should be filled by the most eminent men; and with this object I have invited Mr. Bowditch, of Salem, Massachusetts, to come and occupy the chair of Mathematics, since I consider Mr. Bowditch to be the second mathematician in the world, Laplace being doubtless the first."

"Do you design a Medical Department in the university?"

"I think not. Anatomy, to be sure, is a science; but I have no confidence in *Materia Medica*, which I have long since banished from my family, choosing rather to rely on nursing and nature for a cure. My attention was first called to this subject when I was Minister to France. During my residence in Paris my daughter was seized with a typhus fever, and I sent for a physician, who was called the most eminent and successful one in the city. He came, examined the patient, gave some directions about nursing, and departed, giving no medicine and leaving none to be given. The same course was taken the next day, and the next, when, growing uneasy, I said to him,

" 'Doctor, you don't appear to be doing anything for my daughter. What is the reason?'

" 'The reason is, I wish her to get well. I had supposed you knew what my system of practice was, or you would not have sent for me.'

" 'No; what is it?'

" 'To have the most careful nursing, leave the disease to wear itself out, and let nature do the rest, but give no medicine.'

"Well, Sir, though still uneasy, I acqui-

NEW... ... LIBRARY

NE... ...

29451

esced in the course, and the result was, my daughter recovered with a constitution un-injured by mineral medicine. Since then—a period of nearly thirty years—I have been my own doctor, and scrupulously follow-ing the system of this French physician, have practiced not only in my own family, but among the colored people on my plan-tation, taking them all through the worst of fevers, and never losing a single patient.

"You see," said Mr. Jefferson, after a pause, indicating that he had no more to say on the subject that had been under con-sideration—"you see that ancient looking building down yonder in front of us, a little removed from the foot of this emi-nence? That should be an object of interest to strangers. That was the old home of the noted Patrick Henry."

"It is indeed an object of interest to me, Sir. It would be so at *any* time; and it is especially so at this, as I have just been read-ing Wirt's Life of Henry; and I shall have the opportunity of ascertaining from one,

who is so competent to judge, how far my impression that the biography was over-colored is well grounded."

"In some respects it doubtless *is* over-colored, but in others scarcely colored up to what was the reality. Mr. Wirt makes Henry a statesman and a lawyer: neither of these was true. Henry was a bold and sincere patriot, but no statesman. And his opinion on a law point was absolutely not worth one single brass farthing. But as to the effect of his oratory, Mr. Wirt has hardly done him justice. His power over an audience was wonderful, and to myself, I confess, almost incomprehensible. Men were frenzied under his appeals, and seemed to become the mere machines of his will. I have never witnessed any thing like it either in Europe or America. And I doubt whether there ever was in America any such exhibition of the power of a speaker over an audience, with the exception, perhaps, of Whitfield, the greatest pulpit orator, doubtless, of all modern times. And

Henry, like Whitfield, should have been a preacher. Had he been one, he would have been a prodigy. But what, you will ask, was the secret of this singular power? That is a question which, among thinking men, has before been often asked, but never to my mind satisfactorily answered. It certainly was not from any peculiar richness of thought or force of his ideas; for his speeches when analyzed by the thinking hearer, as soon as he could divest himself of the peculiar effect of their delivery, were seen to amount to but very little. I have myself sat and listened to one of his speeches with a strange thrill of pleasure, yielded myself involuntarily to the influence, shut up my eyes, and sat it out to the end like one in a trance, and then, as I aroused myself from the thrall, I have asked myself, *Now what has the man said to produce such an effect, even on myself, guarded as I was?* But I never could tell. No, that effect was not produced by the force of intellect, but the faculty of completely seizing the sympathies of the hearers, or rather perhaps some magnetic power over them, which was the peculiar gift of the man, and which has been rarely or never possessed by any individual, to the same extent, in this country before. Henry was no scholar, and read scarcely any thing. I recollect he, one fall, came up here, and saying he had been thinking he would read some during the approaching winter, asked me to lend him a book. I lent him a volume of Hume's Essays. He brought it back the next spring, when I asked him if he had read it? 'No,' he replied. 'I tried to read it two or three times, but I never could get through more than a page or so before I fell asleep.' And yet for all his indolence, and his aversion to acquiring what he called book knowledge, Henry had a great soul and a comprehensive intellect, which, on all occasions sufficiently important to arouse his highest faculties, he brought into action with the strength of a giant. Indeed I hardly know what Virginia would have done without the powerful impetus he imparted to the great political revolution of 1776."

"Yes," I here remarked, "Patrick Henry's services in our great political revolution are every where acknowledged; and in reading Wirt's glowing account of those services and of his intense love of freedom, I could not forbear asking an opponent in argument the question I would also like to ask you, and that is, where would Henry, if now alive, with his old keen appreciation of human rights, where would Henry be found in the *social* revolution, or rather the revolution in the domestic institutions of his native State, which, with somewhat divided opinions, you are now inaugurating? —I allude to the institution of slavery, in connection with the State Convention called in part to provide for its gradual abolishment."

"Where would Henry be found, if alive, at this crisis, would you ask? It would require no gift of prophecy in me to answer that question. He would be found with

those with whom, side by side, he once labored in the matter so strenuously—Mr. Madison, myself, and many others of Virginia's most enlightened statesmen. Henry was, at that time, even more determined in his opposition to slavery than the rest of us. The Legislature of Virginia, the first of all the States to take any definite anti-slavery action, as early as 1778, through the influence of Patrick Henry and the few leading men who felt like him, and like him had the moral courage to take a bold and decided stand on the subject, abolished the slave traffic in this State by law. And besides the all-important aid Henry contributed to this measure, he caused his opinions and influence to be heeded and felt by the framers of the Constitution of the United States, an influential portion of whom, under the lead of Mr. Madison, thought that they had so guarded that instrument that it should never afford the remotest sanction to slavery, but rather invite the after prohibitory action of Congress. And when Congress, in response

to our known sentiments, subsequently prohibited the further introduction of slaves
after a certain time, Mr. Madison thought,
and we all thought, we had effectually ac-
complished the great desideratum of giving
slavery its death-blow, or the blow at least
under which the institution could only lin-
ger a few years to perish from the land,
which it had already begun to blight with
its malific influence. But we found ourselves
sadly mistaken. When the time arrived on
which all had counted for its rapid decline,
we saw it taking deeper root than ever. The
cupidity of an influential class, taking ad-
vantage of the thoughtlessness of other
classes, had prevailed. And so it has gone
on, till this terrible incubus on the prosper-
ity and true welfare of the South is swell-
ing up to mountain proportions. This, of
late years, has constituted the burden of my
anxieties; and last spring I had several conversations with Mr. Madison on the subject,
when, finding ourselves perfectly agreed
in views and sentiments, we both resolved

we would make one more effort before we died to rid our State of this unspeakable evil before forever too late. And the result of our movement was the proposition for the gradual emancipation of all the slaves of Virginia, which is soon to be presented for the action of the approaching State Convention for making all expedient alterations in our Constitution, and which, with the strong backing promised us, we have fondly hoped might be adopted. And yet we should not be too sanguine of such an auspicious result. The same causes that have hitherto led to the defeat of every such movement may again conspire to bring this to the same fate, and we shall be compelled to leave the stage of life with our vistas of the earthly future darkened by the presages of the doom, which, if not averted by emancipation, must sooner or later fall, not only on our own beloved State, but the whole South, in the ruin of their people or in the overthrow of their republican liberties, in consequence of the inevitable workings of that most unfortunate institution."

The measure was not destined to prevail, and we are now in a position to estimate the deep foresight embodied in the prophecy of the author of the Declaration of Independence.

This book, designed by R. L. Dothard Associates, has been set by the Pioneer Printing Company of Spofford, N. H. in types cut by Anton Janson in the late Seventeenth Century. It has been printed by the Elm Tree Press of Woodstock, Vt., and bound by the New Hampshire Bindery of Concord.